David Carr Glover
METHOD for PIANO

D0128189

LESSONS

**David Carr Glover
and Jay Stewart**

© 1989 BELWIN-MILLS PUBLISHING CORP.
All Rights Assigned to and Controlled by ALFRED PUBLISHING CO., INC.
All Rights Reserved including Public Performance. Printed in USA.

FOREWORD

Teacher and Parents:

LESSONS, Level Three, from the David Carr Glover METHOD for PIANO reviews the basic concepts presented in LESSONS, Level Two. New concepts are introduced and reinforced sequentially through the use of original compositions, folk songs and the sounds of today. This book, combined with the recommended supplementary materials, continues to assist the student in developing the ability to read and perform musically through interval recognition, sight reading and ear training.

The student will continue to experience the basic elements of improvisation as the creative activities, EXPLORE, are presented.

Supplementary materials are carefully correlated and coded with the LESSONS book to provide reinforcement of all concepts.

The David Carr Glover METHOD for PIANO has been created to provide an educational and pedagogically sound program of piano instruction.

Supplementary materials correlated with
LESSONS, Level Three, from the
David Carr Glover METHOD for PIANO

Contents

Key of _____ , Key Signature _____

THE CAROUSEL

GLOVER - STEWART

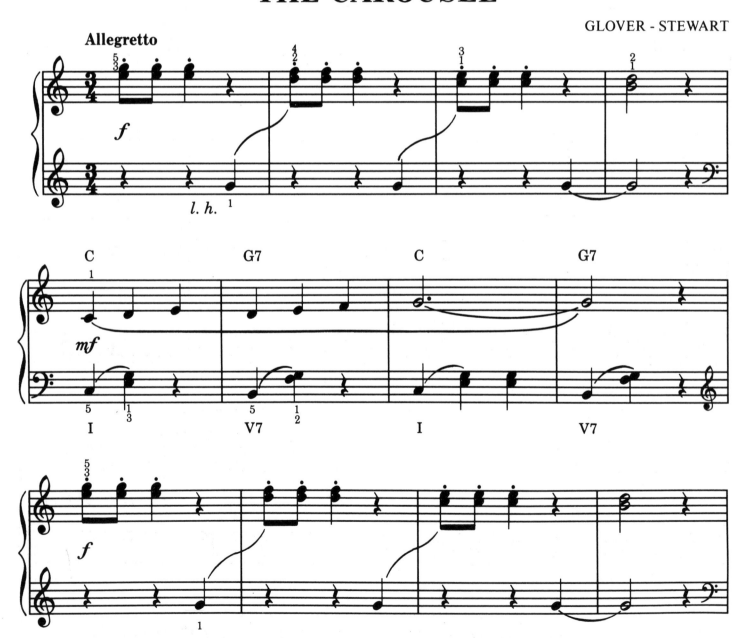

You are now ready for Level Three TECHNIC,
Level Three THEORY, and Level Three SIGHT READING AND EAR TRAINING
from the David Carr Glover METHOD for PIANO.

Key of _____ , Key Signature _____

ARKANSAS TRAVELER

TRADITIONAL

Allegretto

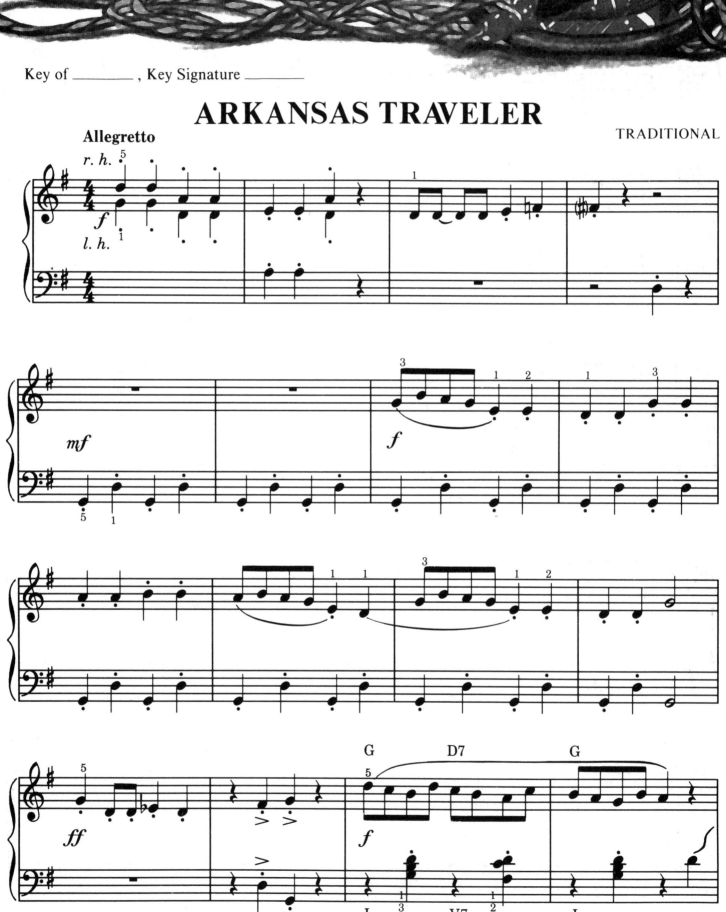

8

TERNARY FORM

A composition consisting of three sections is written in Ternary Form, sometimes referred to as *three part song form*. The first section is referred to as A, the second section is called B, and the third section (which is a repeat of the first section) is also called A. The first four measures of this piece are an Introduction; the last four are a Coda.

Key of _____ , Key Signature _____

THE MARINES' HYMN

PHILLIPS

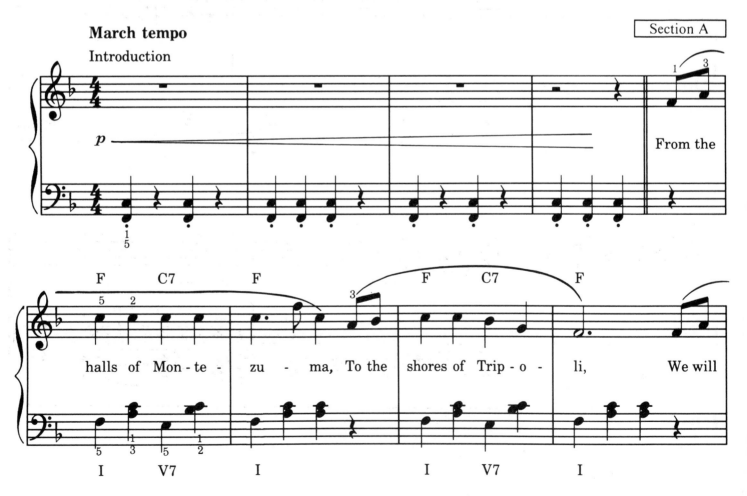

Section B

fight our coun-try's bat - tles, On the land and on the sea. First to

Section A

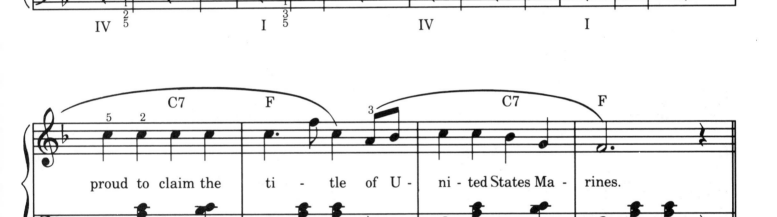

fight for right and free - dom, And to keep our hon - or clean, We are

proud to claim the ti - tle of U - ni - ted States Ma - rines.

Coda

p

EXPLORE: Create a drum accompaniment with your left hand. Play a cluster of the five lowest white keys using this rhythm:
Play the melody as given.

You are now ready for PERFORMANCE, Level Three,
from the David Carr Glover METHOD for PIANO.

Write the letter names of the chords above the treble staff.

Key of _____ , Key Signature _____

THE HOLLY AND THE IVY

OLD ENGLISH TUNE

Lively

The hol-ly and the i-vy, When they are both full grown, Of

I   IV   I   I   IV   I

all the trees that are in the woods, The hol-ly wears the crown.

I   V7   I

Second Part

(Introduction — student begins playing on last beat of measure 4)

Leger Line and Space Notes

LEGER LINES are the short lines added above and below the staff.

Notes which are higher or lower than the staff are placed on leger lines and spaces.

Write the names of the leger notes, then play.

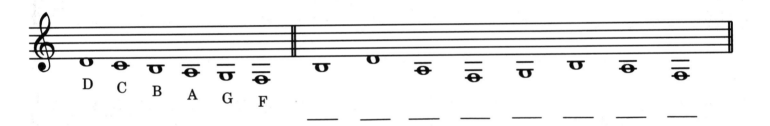

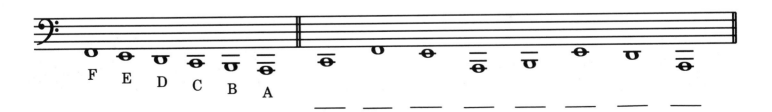

> **sfz** *(sforzando)*
> With a sudden strong accent

LITTLE BROWN JUG

AMERICAN FOLK SONG

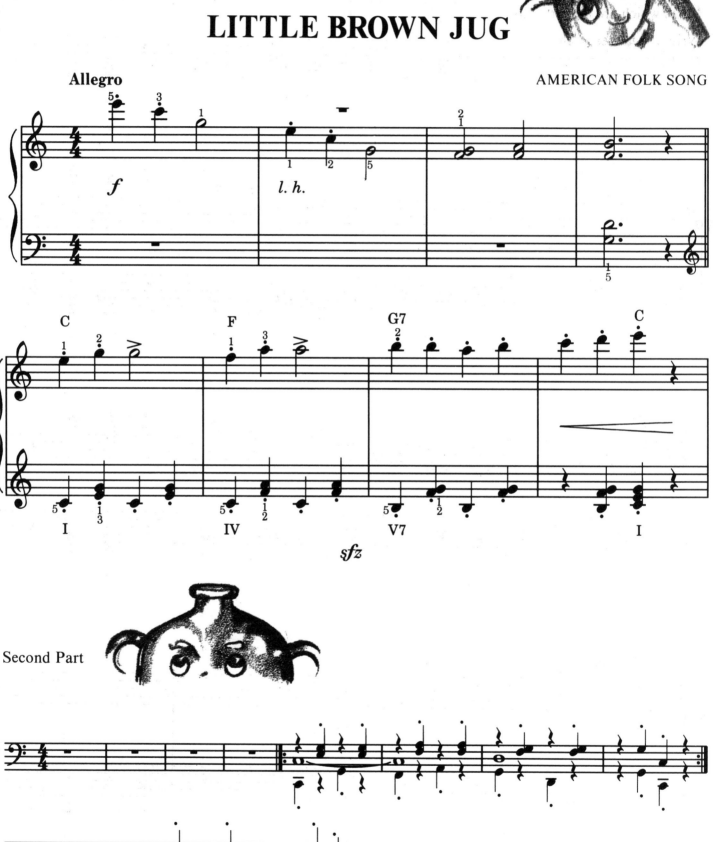

Triplets

A TRIPLET is a group of three notes played in the usual time value of two such notes.

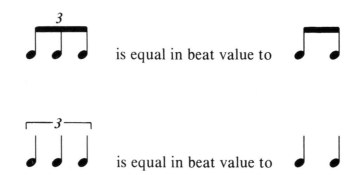

is equal in beat value to

is equal in beat value to

A triplet of eighth notes receives one beat in $\frac{2}{4}$, $\frac{3}{4}$, $\frac{4}{4}$ meter.

Clap and chant this triplet rhythm pattern.

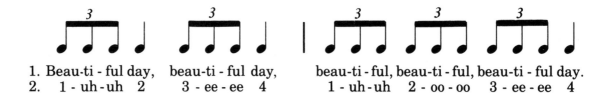

1. Beau-ti-ful day, beau-ti-ful day,   beau-ti-ful, beau-ti-ful, beau-ti-ful day.
2.   1 - uh-uh 2   3 - ee-ee 4   1 - uh-uh   2 - oo-oo   3 - ee-ee   4

Count aloud as you play.

Your teacher will direct you in the preferred method of counting.

I.

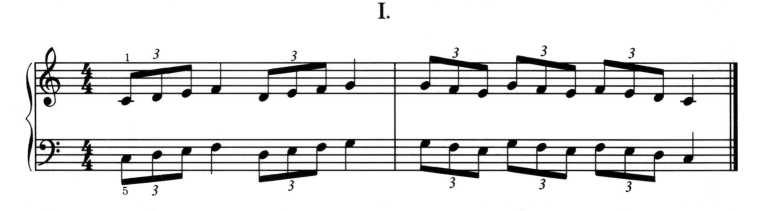

II.

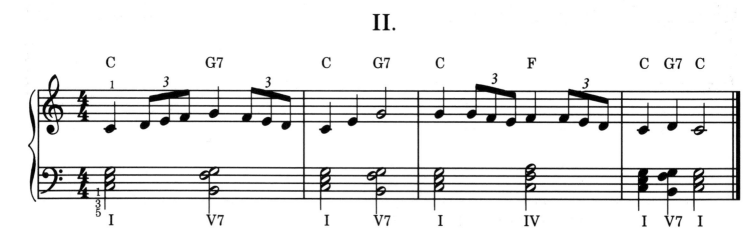

HOUND DOG BLUES

GLOVER - STEWART

EXPLORE: Tap the rhythm of this piece (right hand and left hand together) as you count aloud. Do this activity with several other pieces in this book.

SONG OF THE DESERT

GLOVER - STEWART

Misterioso (with an air of mystery)

Grazioso (gracefully)

EXPLORE: With left hand, play a triplet on beat two of every measure.

SPACE CHASE

GLOVER - STEWART

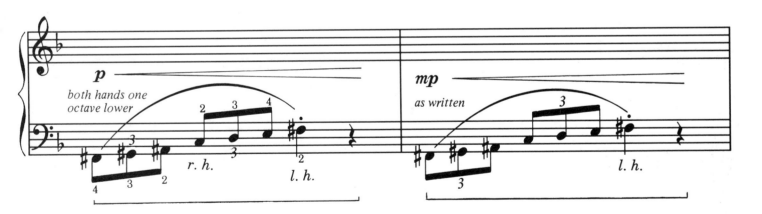

First Inversion Triads

In root position the root is the lowest note of a triad.

ROOT → C E G

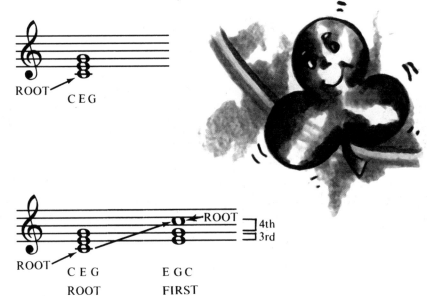

Triads may be INVERTED by moving the root from the bottom to the top.

The intervals change but the note names do not change.

ROOT → C E G
ROOT POSITION

ROOT → E G C
FIRST INVERSION
4th
3rd

Triads in FIRST INVERSION have one interval of a 3rd and one interval of a 4th.

REMEMBER: In first inversion triads the root is at the top of the chord and is the top note of the interval of a 4th.

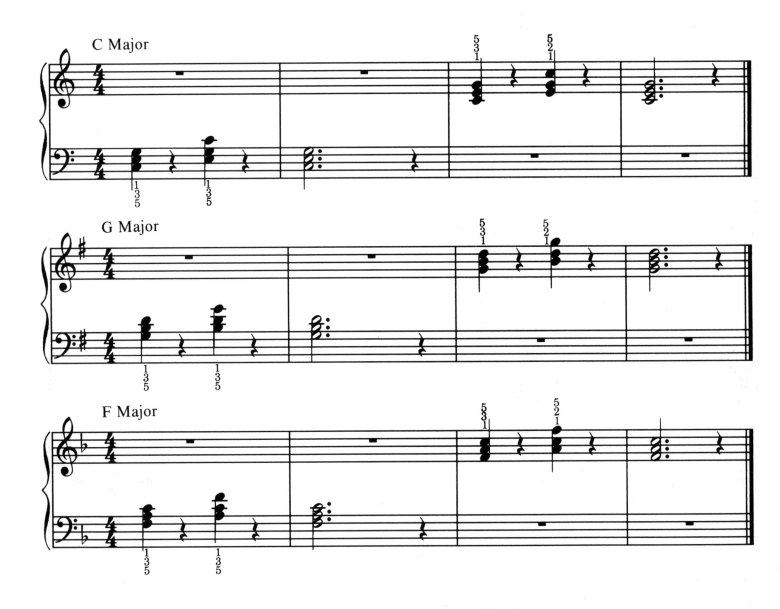

FIRST INVERSION MARCH

GLOVER - STEWART

* *Dal Segno al Fine (D.S. al Fine)* means return to the sign (𝄋) and play to the word *Fine.*

Second Inversion Triads

Remember, a triad may be in first inversion, with the root at the top.

A triad may also be in SECOND INVERSION.

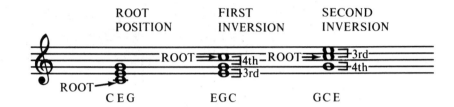

In SECOND INVERSION triads the root is in the middle of the chord and is the higher note of the interval of a 4th. Second inversion triads have one interval of a 4th and one interval of a 3rd.

In FIRST INVERSION triads the root is at the top of the chord and is the higher note of the interval of a 4th. First inversion triads have one interval of a 3rd and one interval of a 4th.

In ROOT POSITION triads the root is always the lowest note.

Play in C Major, then transpose to the key of F Major.

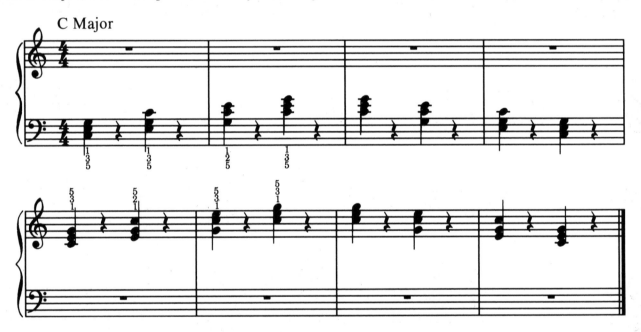

Play in G Major, then transpose to the key of D Major.

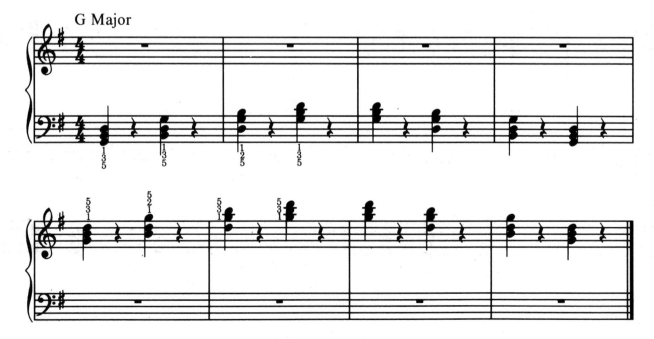

Key of _____ , Key Signature _____

TAPS

TRADITIONAL

Relative Minor Scales

Each major key has a RELATIVE MINOR KEY with the same key signature.

Each RELATIVE MINOR SCALE begins on the 6th degree of the related major scale.

The two scales are related because they share the same key signature.

C MAJOR SCALE

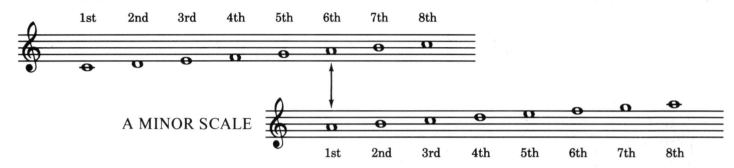

A MINOR SCALE

Forms of the Minor Scales

There are several forms of minor scales, including the NATURAL, the HARMONIC, the MELODIC.

Practice these scales. Play the R.H. as written. Play the L.H. one octave lower than written. Observe the fingering carefully.

1. The NATURAL MINOR SCALE uses the same notes as the relative major scale.

2. The HARMONIC MINOR SCALE uses the same notes as the NATURAL MINOR SCALE, with the exception of the 7th tone which is raised one half step. This raised 7th tone is not included in the key signature.

3. The MELODIC MINOR SCALE uses the same notes as the NATURAL MINOR SCALE, with the exception of the 6th and 7th tones which are raised one half step ASCENDING, then lowered DESCENDING.

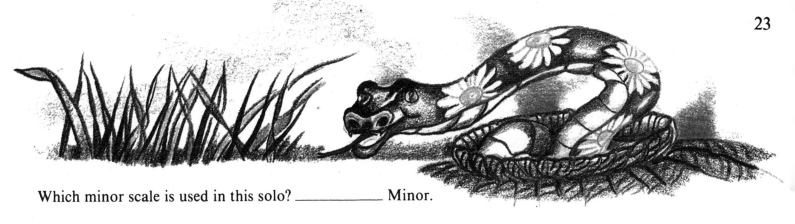

Which minor scale is used in this solo? _____ Minor.

SNAKE IN A BASKET

GLOVER

Key of _____, Key Signature _____

HARVEST DANCE

GLOVER

Lively

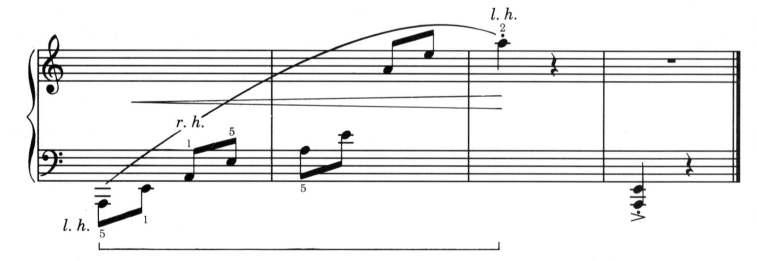

Second Part (Student plays solo one octave higher.)

Major and Minor Triads

MAJOR triads consist of a ROOT and the intervals of a MAJOR 3rd (2 whole steps) and PERFECT 5th (3½ steps) above the root.

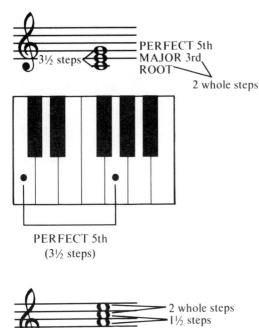

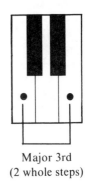

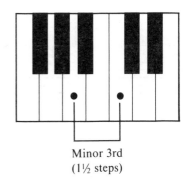

Major 3rd
(2 whole steps)

PERFECT 5th
(3½ steps)

A MINOR triad consists of the first, third, and fifth notes of the minor scale. The minor triad has 1½ steps between the root and the middle note, and 2 whole steps between the middle note and the top note.

MINOR triads consist of a ROOT and the intervals of a MINOR 3rd (1½ steps) and PERFECT 5th (3½ steps) above the root.

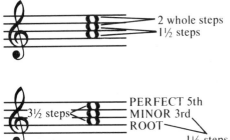

Minor 3rd
(1½ steps)

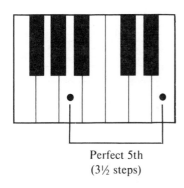

Perfect 5th
(3½ steps)

Any major triad in ROOT POSITION becomes a minor triad when the middle note is lowered one half step.

1. Play each major triad.

2. Change each major triad to a minor triad by lowering the middle note one half step.

3. Play each minor triad.

4. Change each minor triad to a major triad by raising the middle note one half step.

GREENSLEEVES

Moderato

ENGLISH FOLK SONG

EXPLORE: Play all of the left hand accompaniment in broken chords,
then play all of the left hand accompaniment in block chords.

Primary Chords In Minor Keys

PRIMARY CHORDS in minor keys are formed by using the notes of the HARMONIC MINOR scale. The 7th note of the scale is raised one half step.

Lower case Roman numerals are used to indicate the minor triads (i, iv).
Lower case m after the chord letter name indicates a minor chord (Am = A Minor).

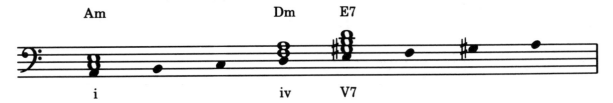

In minor keys the i and iv chords are minor chords.
The V7 chord is always a major chord.
Minor chords, like major chords, can be inverted.

Practice the following A Harmonic Minor scale, chord progression and arpeggio.
Observe the fingering carefully.

A Harmonic Minor Scale

A Minor Chord Progression

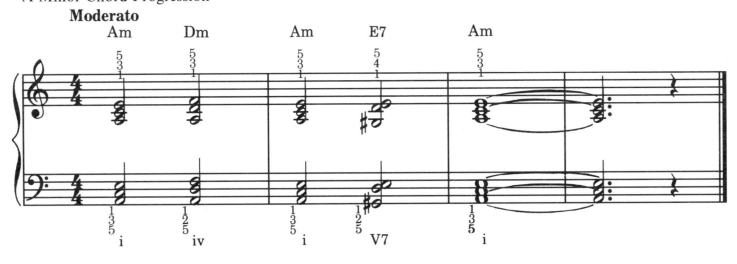

A Minor Arpeggio

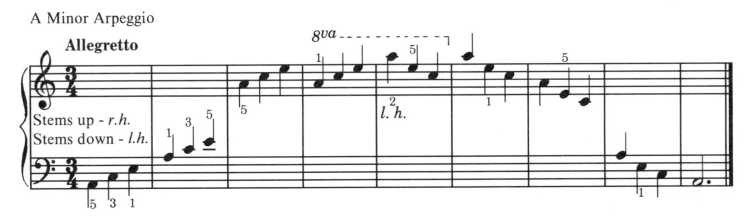

On page 20, transpose the given major triads and inversions to minor keys.

THE LONELY SHEPHERD

Key of _____ , Key Signature _____

GLOVER

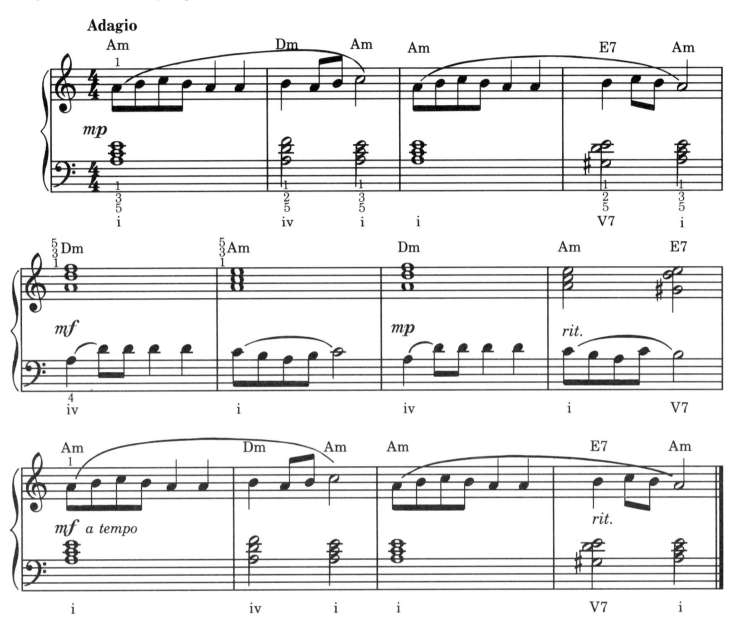

EXPLORE: Tap the rhythm of this piece (right hand and left hand together) as you count aloud. Do this activity with several other pieces in this book.

Second Part

8va throughout

Stephen Foster (1826-1864) was an American composer. His songs were very popular in nineteenth century America. Some of his most beloved songs are *Swanee River*, *Jeanie with the Light Brown Hair*, *Beautiful Dreamer* and *Camptown Races*.

OH! SUSANNA

STEPHEN FOSTER

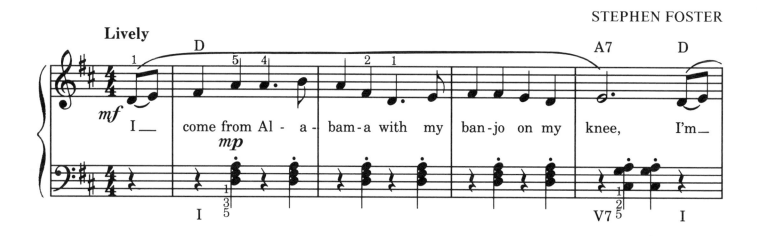

I __ come from Al - a - bam-a with my ban-jo on my knee, I'm __

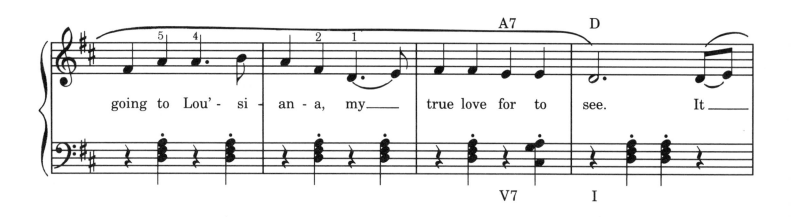

going to Lou' - si - an - a, my __ true love for to see. It __

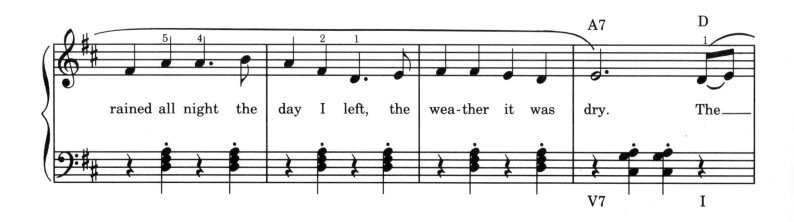

rained all night the day I left, the wea-ther it was dry. The __

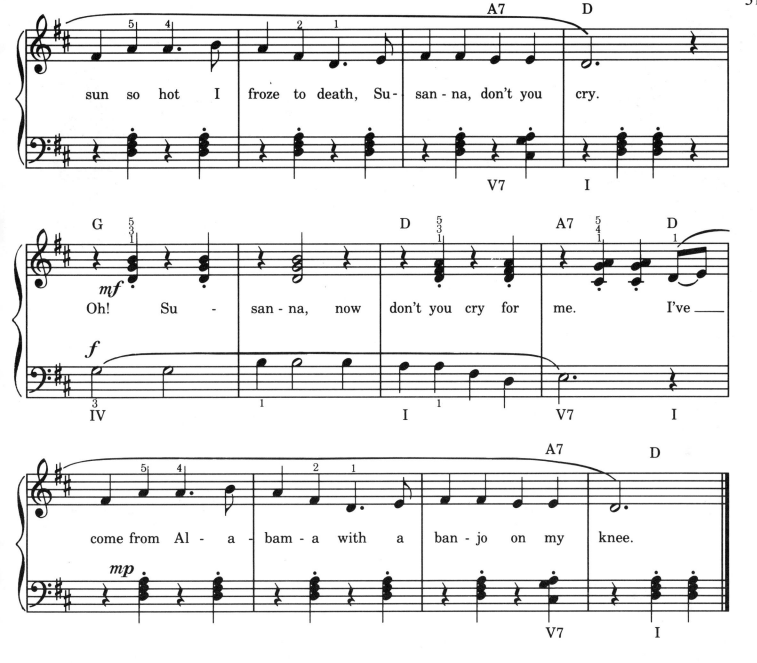

EXPLORE: Play the left hand accompaniment of this piece as you sing the melody (words or note names). **DO NOT** play the right hand. For excellent ear training, do this activity with several other pieces in this book.

Second Part (Student plays solo one octave higher.)

(Oh! Su - san - na, now, don't you cry for me.)

SARASPONDA

TRADITIONAL

Animato (lively, animated)

EXPLORE: Change the left hand accompaniment to block chords.
Play the last 4 measures as written.

etc.

COMPUTE-A-BOOGIE

Fast and mechanically

GLOVER - STEWART

EXPLORE: Play the right hand legato.

$\frac{6}{8}$ Time Signature

6 ⟶ Beats to each measure

8 ⟶ Each eighth note receives one beat.

Notes	Beats	Rests	Clap once for each note as you count aloud.

1. Clap and count aloud. Do not clap on the rests.

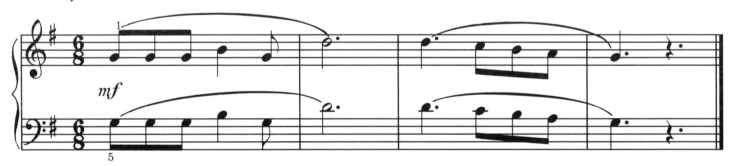

2. Play and count aloud.

Key of _____ , Key Signature _____

LOOBY LOO

TRADITIONAL

Allegretto

cresc. *(crescendo):*
gradually louder

dim. *(diminuendo):*
gradually softer

Notice that the left hand part
is written high in the treble
clef for the introduction.

WHEN JOHNNY COMES MARCHING HOME

TRADITIONAL

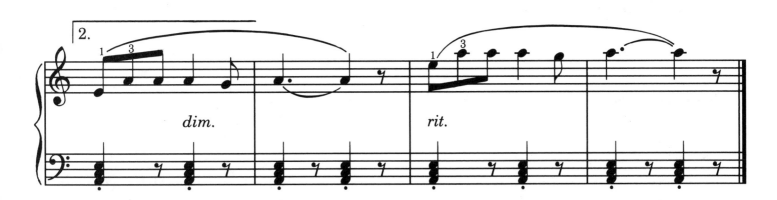

EXPLORE: Play the following accompaniment throughout with the left hand.

Key of D Minor

Remember that each major key has a relative minor key with the same key signature. A relative minor scale begins on the 6th degree of the related major scale. The two scales are related because they share the same key signature.

F MAJOR SCALE

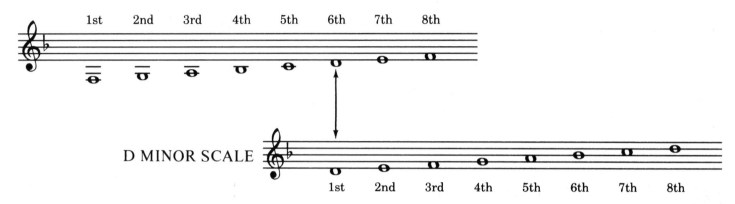

Forms of the Minor Scale (Review)

There are several kinds of minor scales, including the NATURAL, the HARMONIC, the MELODIC. Practice these scales. Play the R.H. as written. Play the L.H. one octave lower than written.

1. The NATURAL MINOR SCALE uses the same notes as the relative major scale.

2. The HARMONIC MINOR SCALE uses the same notes as the NATURAL MINOR SCALE with the exception of the 7th tone which is raised one half step. This raised 7th tone is not in the key signature.

3. The MELODIC MINOR SCALE uses the same notes as the NATURAL MINOR SCALE with the exception of the 6th and 7th tones which are raised one half step ASCENDING, then lowered DESCENDING.

Key of _____ , Key Signature _____

SONG OF THE NILE

GLOVER - STEWART

Primary Chords in D Minor

Remember: Primary chords in a minor key are formed by using the notes of the HARMONIC MINOR scale. The 7th tone of the scale is raised one half step.

Lower case Roman numerals are used to indicate the minor triads (i, iv).

Lower case m after the chord letter name indicates a minor chord (Dm = D minor).

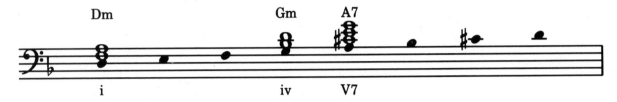

In minor keys the i and iv chords are minor chords.

The V7 chord is always a major chord.

Minor chords, like major chords, can be inverted.

Practice the following D Harmonic Minor scale, chord progression and arpeggio.
Observe the fingering carefully.

D Harmonic Minor scale.

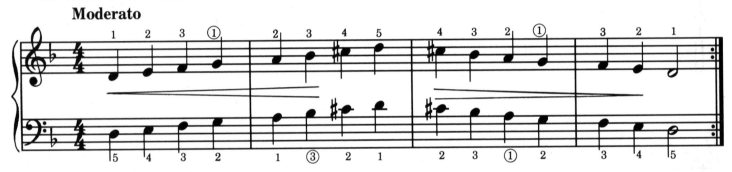

D Minor Chord Progression

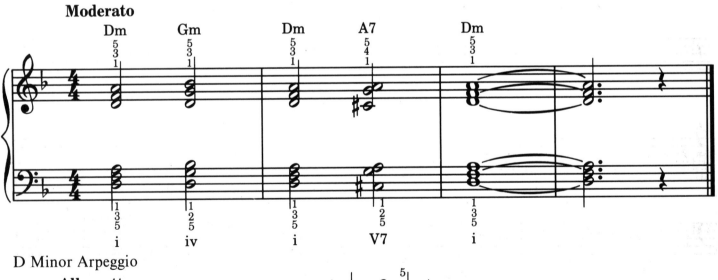

D Minor Arpeggio

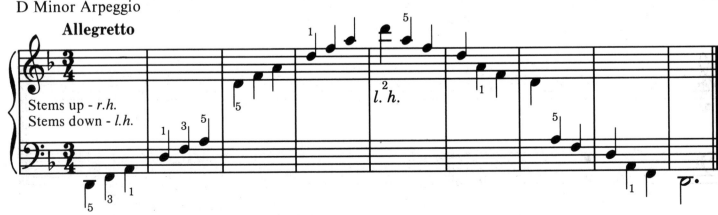

Write the letter names of the chords above the treble staff.

VIDEO GAME

GLOVER - STEWART

Key of _____ , Key Signature _____

MINKA

FOLK SONG

More About the Damper Pedal

This pedal sign means to lift the damper pedal
and then press it down again immediately.

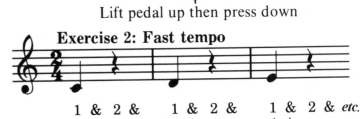

Press down ➔ Lift up ◄

Lift pedal up then press down

Exercise 1: Slow tempo

1 2 3 4   1 2 3 4   1 2 3 4 *etc.*

Exercise 2: Fast tempo

1 & 2 &   1 & 2 &   1 & 2 & *etc.*

(Pedal marks are written in various ways. This kind, with space between, is the mark most often used for
pedal exercises.)

1. First play hands separately, one octave, using finger 3.
2. Play hands together, one octave, using finger 3.
3. (optional) Play triads on each scale degree.

Remember to keep your heel on the floor with the ball of your foot ALWAYS touching the pedal.

ETUDE

GLOVER - STEWART

SPANISH GUITAR

STEWART

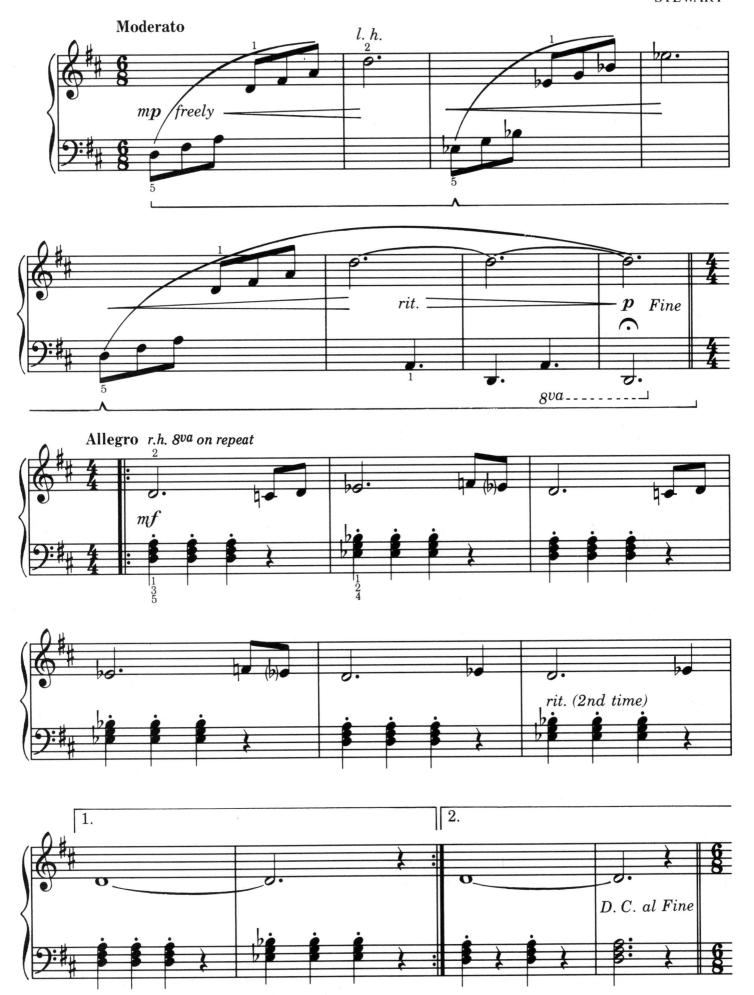

Syncopation

SYNCOPATION is a shifting of the normal accent.
When a long note is played on the weak part of the beat, a form of syncopation occurs.

Clap and count aloud this rhythm pattern.

I.

Allegretto

II.

Allegretto

SYNCOPATED RAG

Key of _____ , Key Signature _____

This style of music was introduced in the late 1800s and is known as RAGTIME.

GLOVER - STEWART

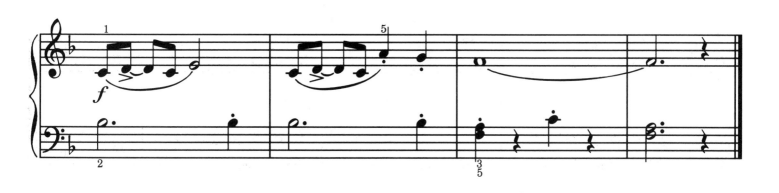

Scott Joplin (1868-1917) was born in Texarkana, Texas. The young lad spent much time at the piano and he became a fine improviser. A local music teacher recognized Scott's outstanding talent and gave him free piano lessons. Joplin composed many syncopated piano solos called rags. Two of his most famous are *Maple Leaf Rag* and *The Entertainer*. Joplin also wrote a black folk opera, *Treemonisha*.

THE ENTERTAINER

Key of _____ , Key Signature _____

SCOTT JOPLIN

Chromatic Scale

The CHROMATIC SCALE is a series of twelve successive half steps.
It may begin on any note. It does not have a key signature.

CHROMATIC SCALE FINGERING

1. Use finger 3 on all black keys.
2. Use finger 1 on all white keys
   except when two white keys are
   played successively, then use
   fingers 1 and 2 or 2 and 1.

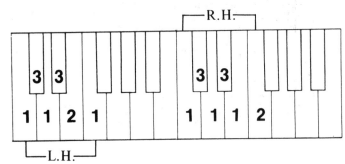

1. Practice the fingering shown on the keyboard above, ascending and descending.
2. Practice the chromatic scale below, hands separately, then hands together.

JOSHUA FOUGHT THE BATTLE OF JERICHO

Allegretto

SPIRITUAL

Whole Tone Scale

The WHOLE TONE SCALE consists of six successive whole steps. Debussy, a nineteenth century French writer, used the whole tone scale in many of his compositions.

Locate the WHOLE TONE SCALES in "The Secret Sea."

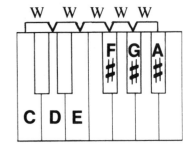

| C (Common time) |
| a way to indicate $\frac{4}{4}$ time |

THE SECRET SEA

Adagio

GLOVER - STEWART

Write the Roman numerals of the chords below the bass staff.

AULD LANG SYNE

TRADITIONAL

simile (continue in the same pattern)

Review

1. Before each music symbol or word (Column 2), write the number of the correct definition (Column 1).

Column 1   Column 2

   1. Series of twelve successive half steps   _____ *pp*

   2. Pedal sign: Lift pedal up, then press down   _____ *sfz*

   3. Time signature: 6 beats to each measure;
      each eighth note receives one beat   _____ Triplet

   4. A shifting of the normal accent   _____ Misterioso

   5. With spirit   _____ D.S. al Fine

   6. *Pianissimo:* very soft   _____ $\frac{6}{8}$

   7. *Sforzando:* with a strong accent   _____ Con brio

   8. *Fortissimo:* very loud   _____ ⌐∧⌐

   9. A group of three notes played in the usual
      time value of two such notes   _____ Syncopation

  10. With an air of mystery   _____ Chromatic scale

  11. *Dal Segno al Fine:* return to the sign (𝄋)
      and play to the word *fine* (pronounced
      Fee-nay)   _____ *ff*

2. Name each melodic and harmonic interval. Play each interval.

3. Write key names, chord symbols and Roman numerals for the following chord progressions.

Key _____   Key_____

Chord
symbol __   __   __   __   __   __   __   __   __   __

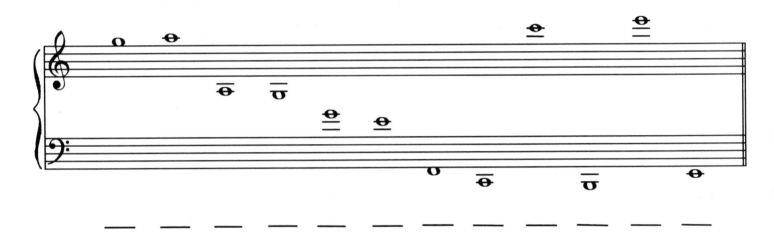

Roman
numeral __   __   __   __   __   __   __   __   __   __

4. Write the names of the leger notes, then play.

__   __   __   __   __   __   __   __   __   __

Music Dictionary

MUSICAL TERM	ABBREVIATION or SIGN	DEFINITION
Accent	>	To make louder
Adagio		Slowly, between largo and andante
Alla marcia		In march time
Allegretto		A little slower than allegro
Allegro		Fast, brisk
Andante		A walking tempo
Animato		Lively
A tempo		Return to original tempo
Chromatic scale		A series of twelve successive half steps
Coda		An added ending
Con brio		With spirit
Crescendo	*Cresc.*	Gradually louder
Da capo al fine	*D.C. al fine*	Return to the beginning and repeat to the word *fine*
Dal segno al fine	*D.S. al fine*	Return to the sign (𝄋) and repeat to the word *fine*
Decrescendo	*Decresc.*	Gradually softer
Diminuendo	*Dim.*	Gradually softer
Fermata	⌢	Hold or pause
Forte	*f*	Loud
Fortissimo	*ff*	Very loud
Grazioso		Gracefully
Harmonic minor scale		Begins on the 6th degree of its related major scale (same key signature), with the 7th tone raised one-half step
Inverted triads		Triad with the root as the top note or middle note of the chord
Legato		Smooth and connected
Leger lines		Added lines and spaces above and below the staff
Melodic minor scale		Begins on the 6th tone of its related major scale (same key signature), with the 6th and 7th tones raised one half step ascending, then lowered descending
Mezzo forte	*mf*	Moderately loud
Mezzo piano	*mp*	Moderately soft
Minor triad		Consists of a root and the intervals of a minor 3rd (1½ steps) and a perfect 5th (3½ steps) above the root

Misterioso	With an air of mystery
Moderato	A moderate speed
Molto	Much or very
Natural minor scale	Begins on the 6th degree of its related major scale (same key signature) and uses the same tones
Ottava ... *8va* ...	When *8va* is placed OVER a note or group of notes, it means to play 8 keys (one octave) higher than written. When *8va* is placed UNDER the notes, it means to play 8 keys lower
Perfect fifth	Interval of a fifth comprised of 3½ steps
Pianissimo ... *pp* ...	Very soft
Piano ... *p* ...	Soft
Presto	Very fast
Primary chords	Triads built on the first, fourth and fifth degrees of the scale
Relative minor scale	Scale related to the major scale through sharing the same key signature; begins on the 6th tone of the related major scale
Repeat sign	To play over again
Ritardando ... *rit.* ...	Gradually slowing
Sforzando ... *sfz.* ...	With a sudden strong accent
Simile	Continue the same
Staccato ... *stacc.* ...	Short, disconnected
Syncopation	Shifting of the normal accent; a weak beat functioning as a strong beat
Triplet	A group of three notes played in the usual time value of two such notes
Ternary form	A composition in three sections, A-B-A
Whole tone scale	A scale using only whole steps, six to the octave

Certificate of Accomplishment

This certifies that

_____

has completed

LESSONS,
LEVEL THREE
of the

David Carr Glover

METHOD for PIANO
and is promoted to LEVEL FOUR

_____
(Teacher)

_____
(Date)